Reverberations

Reverberations

Poems by

Kim Malinowski

© 2025 Kim Malinowski. All rights reserved.
This material may not be reproduced in any form, published,
reprinted, recorded, performed, broadcast,
rewritten, or redistributed without
the explicit permission of Kim Malinowski.
All such actions are strictly prohibited by law.

Cover design by Shay Culligan
Cover image by Bryan C. Smith
Author photo by Bryan C. Smith

ISBN: 978-1-63980-741-3
Library of Congress Control Number: 2025936279

Kelsay Books
502 South 1040 East, A-119
American Fork, Utah 84003
Kelsaybooks.com

Acknowledgments

Thank you to the following publications, in which versions of these poems previously appeared:

Golden Walkman Magazine: "Trzy Tysiące Pięćset Sześćdziesiąt Trzy" originally published as "Ignored Numeral"
Mad Poets Review: "Dziadek" originally published as "Grandfather"
The Sunlight Magazine: "Miya-Jima"
War, Literature, & the Arts: "Great Uncle"
Words & Whispers: "Babushka"

I would like to thank my parents, Ty Chadwell-English and his family, Sarah Criscuolo, and Kathryn Barrow for their endless support. I am grateful to Bryan C. Smith for his superb photography skills and his willingness to allow my chaos into his world. I would like to thank Myra Sklarew and Kyle Dargan for being on my thesis committee. I also must acknowledge my former professors at West Virginia University where I began this project including Lisa Weihman, Patrick Conner, Kevin Oderman, and Gail Galloway Adams for their mentorship and support. I am grateful to Scott Allen who allowed me to use his name despite his discomfort and it being "really weird" in becoming part of a metanarrative within the vast narrative of atrocity.

I am grateful to everyone that remembers their ancestors, learns history, and creates change. We will hold each other with our generational losses and give each other hope for the future. It cannot be denied that we have looped back eighty years. The rhetoric is the same, as is the question each of my friends asks themselves. Will they "toe the line" or will they rebel? No one asks me because they know that I'm not a "toe the line" person. It's my ink you want so that your children will remember the current evils in the years to come. Each person survives and makes the decisions they need for their family and for their careers. I honor each person's individual choice. But, make no mistake, I will be the voice of resistance and history for as long as I am allowed, but you may be called to take my place and step forward past the toe line. Persevere.

Contents

Excavation	15
Najazd	16
Artifacts	17
Transecting	18
Łamany	19
Babushka	20
Dziadek	21
Rozgoryczenie	22
Trzy Tysiące Pięćset Sześćdziesiąt Trzy	23
Sampling	24
Hedgerows	25
Great Uncle	26
Obstrzał	27
Nieznany	28
Provenance	29
Kochanka	30
Żołnierze	32
Soldaten	33
Shwule	34
Seriation	36
Powracać	41
Matka Polka	42
Recording	44
To the Unknown Artist	45
Monologue of a Nazi/German Denier	46
Shoah	47
Churban	48
Assemblage	49
Страстное желание	50
Чувство собственного достоинства	51
Routine	52
Russian Sniper	53

In the Sunshine	54
Remembering	55
The Named	56
Preparation	57
Urban Archeology	58
Ambush	59
Rasputitsa Began	60
Cierpienie	61
Sifting	62
Разрушение	63
Miya-Jima	64
Mr. Yu	65
Reverberations	66
Author Notes	69
Title Translations	71

War does not determine who is right—only who is left.

—Bertrand Russell

Excavation

I sat beside Scott, glancing
at the books on the wooden table.
He smelled of dust and old leather.
I had an ink smudge staining my left cheek,
silence broken only by the pen scratching
against the paper, his soft breathing,
pages turning. He pointed to a passage
he'd highlighted. I leaned in, reading
half over his shoulder, our fingers tracing
over it, as if absorbing the past.

Najazd

It was September 1, 1939, when the Germans invaded the border. We huddled around the radio, waiting for our favorite program, when the alert went out. The first week we heard how brave the military was, how the men were in high spirits and sure to win. And then the Russians entered from the East. The defeats mounted. The borders closed. September 28, 1939, Warsaw fell, few units held out until October.

Artifacts

They didn't tell me.
Books hinted at it—told me dates. Places.
There are yellowing family pictures.
A woman in a gray shawl, a man in a long coat.
Strangers. I don't know their real names.
They fled Poland—survived.
Generations later, I have questions
only the dead can answer.

Transecting

We don't talk about it because we are ashamed,
we just haven't decided why yet.
We're ashamed of being illegal, guilty
because we didn't stay and suffer.
The silence is a clinging presence,
every time I mention the war
or our family, my father cries.

How can I remember if I'm not told the stories?

This is what I know.

>My great-uncle gave my great-grandfather
>his passport so that he could escape Poland.
>
>My great-uncle sailed to Canada. He walked
>and hitchhiked through the countryside,
>snuck into America.
>
>He met back up with my great-grandfather in
>Pittsburgh.
>
>My great-Aunt was tattooed in a concentration
>camp.

This is all that I know.

Łamany

for my Great Aunt

She was half a woman, when released,
spoke in whispers, eyes silent and gray.
She was pale and thin,
her glassy eyes shielded her,
a number tattooed on her right arm spoke for her.
She wore a drab gray homespun dress,
had a soft washed-out beauty.
Sometimes she would call out
to people we couldn't see.
She would speak in Polish,
her voice a cracked violin song.

Babushka

My great-grandmother stared at the crossroads before her,
traffic passing by thick and heavy. She closed her eyes
chin towards heaven, singing an old Polish hymn,
stepped out in front of the cars, steadily weaving
between without a thought.

She asked her husband for money to get groceries.
He yelled about how much she spent, how hard
he worked, berated her for her service. But she
straightened out her stooped back and held out her hand.
When he ignored her, she waved it. He nodded at her.
"Fine!" he yelled, but took out his wallet, and threw
a few bills onto the floor. He spat and harrumphed,
went into the living room, carrying the plate of cookies
she'd baked. She shook her head.

Her American daughter-in-law, told her
she didn't have to put up with him. She wanted nothing
to do with that American-ness, nothing at all.
She liked his hardness, his unbending.
She yelled at her to stop meddling in her marriage.
The girl was shocked, stared as she went out the door.

She coached her daughter-in-law in cooking,
each limp noodle, each broken dish,
apple pie covered the floor, the girl was witched.
She gently explained the way cabbage should look,
fresh and deep green, even when boiled.
Her hands kneaded the bread.

Dziadek

I remember the dust-covered piano,
dirt floors, the wood-burning heater,
the taste of venison in spaghetti sauce,
but I cannot remember his voice.
I imagine that it was gruff—thick with accent.
He was tall and hard,
would lift his cane like a barbell.
I dangled from it, giggling—
captured in a yellowing photograph.
Even then, his eyes were shadowed.
The silence of my father,
is the silence of my great-grandfather.
We do not speak.

Rozgoryczenie

A small Polish city, crowded, borders contracting,
fear mixed with sweat and defiance. Babushkas crying
for Cecylia taken in an alley by a nameless German,
torn dress, bloody smudges, dirty, tear-tracked cheeks.
For Marja raped and shot by a fur-covered Slav,
left to freeze, while her parents watched, unable to bury her.
For Anna, Irina, and Olenka, whose uncles and brothers
held them in the dark beneath sweaty covers.
Rotten trash littered the streets, silence broken by gunfire.
A list of names called out by an officer,
young men led onto wagons bound for war.
The blondes sent away, the darker ones left to work or die.
Even the snakes hid in the corners.

Trzy Tysiące Pięćset Sześćdziesiąt Trzy

They crossed out her name, etched a number on her arm,
took her long blue dress, her bracelet, her children,
grazed a rusty razor across her scalp, held her down on a table
and spread her legs, tracing each fold.

She worried about the food, the poisons in it,
tried fasting but gave up after three days.
Soldiers came and went, never looking at her face.

She tried everything to keep her breasts pert, when no one
was looking she flexed her muscles, watched other women get
    older,
their breasts sagging, the number of men using them dwindled.
She watched them lead out. Knew they were gone with the others.

When the blood came it was a relief, the soldiers didn't understand
    her tears.
They beat her, heavy blows, fists pounding on her back,
"Dirty, dirty, all of you just like animals."
They beat her as she wiped the ground, smearing blood in circles.

Sampling

I was rambling about trenches, surrounded by notes,
and Scott shook his head and muttered "hedgerows."
I raised an eyebrow and continued on,
making sure to emphasize "trenches" each time.
Again, he shook his head.
"No," he explained, "not trenches, hedgerows."
"H.E.D.G.E. rows?"
"Yes, like a bush. They were in World War II.
Trenches were primarily used in World War I."
And then his blue eyes opened wider, brighter,
shutters suddenly opening. He began quickly
detailing the entire Normandy invasion,
the hedgerows, weird mazelike bushes,
their role for the Germans, the Cullen tank
that opened them up, and then, as if he had said too much,
he fell silent.
His eyes shadowed over.

Hedgerows

It surrounded them, like a forest, green
dense leaves, shrouding the enemy. They peered
through the underbrush, waiting for a glimpse of fabric,
of flesh, a glint of a barrel. They cut through
the mazes, with knives and sheers. Tanks
slowly making tunnels, collapsing the terraces
as swarms of Americans advanced,
stepping over bodies.

Great Uncle

Glen was a digger, a tunneler,
he was good at what he did, enjoyed it even.
He was wounded three times and kept going back.
He liked the monotony, it allowed him to think,
to hear the music in his head.
He was the group's listener because he had perfect pitch,
each bomb's whine was just a little bit different,
enough to bet his life on.
He wasn't wrong those three times, just unlucky.

He loved the dirt, the coarseness of it,
the subtly of texture.
He crawled inch-by-inch in the darkness,
dirt pressing on all sides,
barely contained explosions causing dirt to shift.
His heartbeat louder than the thundering above him,
enemy voices echoed in nearby shafts,
the vibrations faint but distinct,
everything was muted,
reality seemed damp and distorted.

After the war, he wasn't the same,
He painted the insides of airplane wings,
each layer three millimeters thick, yellow,
without smudge marks, or imperfections.
No creativity or variation,
inside the wing was comforting
like the tunnels, quiet.

Obstrzał

They heard gunfire in the distance,
booms of thunder, the air was thick
and smothering with soot, fog.
The closer they got to the front, the more dust
they breathed. Trees were cracked and bent,
others cut off stumps. Polish horses in death throes,
their masters lay beneath them. Everything was desolate,
a few clumps of grass, a few surviving trees,
the cat they found by the mortar, sheen of blood on damp fur.

Nieznany

Without names or faces
silenced voices in a burning barn,
wood soaked in gasoline, ignition.
Soldiers spit on the crossroads.
Priests and Boy Scouts marched
into the cold and shot.
Blackened faces, cut-out people.
like names chipped off gravestones,
people erased.

Provenance

Remembering is much like clasping fog
grasping ether
as you lay on a grave picking grass,
the touch of the tombstone—damp
his face fleeting . . .

The laughter of the blue-eyed man
as you wrestled both falling
into a jumble of limbs.

It is an embrace
inhaling existence
the particular taste of strawberries
one Friday in January.

Caressing the painful
stories merge
my story
my people's story
inhabits me.
The taste of blood and dirt
caked sweat of war
putting layers upon layers on
forgetting is too easy.

Kochanka

I glanced at a woman who reminded me of her.
I watched them undress her, watched them beat her
but it wasn't Shaya. Who knows . . . she could be dead.
I remember us together, her chest bruising against mine,
her dark hair tumbling as I took out the bobby pins,
unbraiding it. She was naked and smiling
as I kissed her. I laid her on the bed, kissing
each cheek, a quick brush against her mouth.
and then trailing down her breasts and her stomach,
hands twisted in hair. She smelled of berries and honey
and the musky scent of arousal. I see her eyes
in my dreams, deep umber eyes haunting.

She visited me ghostlike,
her long hair hanging forward.
I couldn't understand her whispers
only her hand tangling in my hair
her kiss searing me.
I woke gasping—fear clenching
my stomach tight.
She could be anywhere.

Shaya was dead?
A friend told me—she'd seen it,
watched her die.
She said it was painless
but she lied.
So, she was gone then—dead.
For a whole year.
She shifted in my memory,

her features blurring like my mother and brother.
My friend gave me a few beads, a small stone,
that Shaya had saved.

She liked moss and ferns,
the red of sunsets,
making love on a blanket under the tree
in the backyard,
red wine, shell lipstick,
her kisses burned.

Żołnierze

They sat around the fire, wrote
letters to their mothers, to their girlfriends,
listened for news about the front,
their hometown, the dead.
Roll call would get shorter and then longer
once the new recruits came.
They loved their God, loved their country,
hated the Germans, whose
humanity mocked their own.
They slept to a hymn of bombshells,
woke in fear when it fell silent,
the smoke hanging like fog,
they shivered until another bomb hit nearby.

Soldaten

They sat around the fire, sipped old dusty liquor
inherited from a dead man, they wore his socks too.
They drank to his health and laughed,
spat in the dirt, trying to get rid of the taste.
They praised Hitler as drunk as they were, blessed him and cooed
a love song, laughing throatily.
They loved their country, they'd forgotten
the slight shadow cast by the hill by their town, forgotten
the houses, the dogs, themselves,
they polished their boots, shivered in the Polish night.

Shwule

He walked into the camp, had a slight swagger,
knew that even in faded trousers he looked
tempting. He saw the guards watching, knew they
were imagining him thrown roughly from bed,
his lover cringing as the police hit him,
screaming *Arschficker,*
and yet, he knew they wanted him.

They watched him as he entered
with the other men, stared at his ass
as he sauntered, at the seductive
curve of his abdomen.
He was well fed,
had dark curls and was tan.
He smiled at them, leered, taunted them,
practically begged them to come.

Some were sent out to the cement works,
others to medical labs. But he was lucky,
knew that he was lucky and that was why
the others hated him. A guard stepped
away from the shadows and asked if he wanted
to go with him. "Of course," he nodded. Clearly
there was no option. He was ushered away.
Undressed in a nearby room, the guard slid his penis in
using only spit and grinding, but he was safe.

Later, he sat in the corner of the cell,
his legs drawn up, his arms hugging them,
his chin tightly pressed.
He was staring at the door.
He was grateful, certainly, but felt lost even with
his lover, his tormentor, protector.
They knew why he got better food,
why he didn't have tattered clothes,
he wasn't dirty and starved—and honestly,
he'd hate himself too.

He was tired, and cold, and really, where was Stan?
He should have come an hour ago . . ..
But maybe he was sick or dead or lost interest . . .
And then what? The cement yard?

He started gasping for air,
unaware of his rocking,
sweat beaded his forehead.
Stan entered, smelling of gunpowder and oil,
drew him off of the ground and wrapped
himself around him until the shivering stopped.
"Shhh," he cooed, "I've got you."

Seriation

He was a soldier,
had on the typical
German uniform.

                                                A field gray tunic,
                                                black pebbled jack boots

size 9

                                                . . .

He was 17 pretending to be 19.

                                                They needed willing men.

He was average, had dirty hands.

                                                Blonde hair, bluish eyes.

Good enough to be a soldier.

                                              He carried a canteen, a
                                              shaving kit, three
                                              photographs, fear.

Would do anything for his fuehrer.

                              He held a Mauser K-98.

It was slender, had a deep oak hue.

                              He had a mole above his
                              upper lip.

When he was nervous, he'd rub it.
He stood before a motley group
of refugees.

                              They weren't refugees.
                              They were prisoners.
                              They wore Ps,
                              Pink Triangles,
                              Stars of David.

Regardless, they weren't really there.

                              Just his imagination, but he
                              could feel them staring at
                              him.

Every time he closed his eyes—bullet
holes and cracked skulls—wounds
reached out.

                              He had shot them. Lined
                              them up. Divided them . . .

camps, fires, gas chambers . . .
They haunted him. In his dreams
they were screaming.

                                        It was 1943.
                                        He was in Poland.

Girls with broken dolls.
Dead fathers, grandmothers . . .

Angry babushkas chanting dead curses.
He was just following orders.

                                        He was dirty, tired, ashamed.

He had his duty and didn't question,
didn't run from battle.

Would you question them?

                                        . . . yes. Of course.
                                        That's why we're not
                                        soldiers.

Hypothetically though?

                                        I wouldn't run from battle.
                                        That doesn't mean I'd
                                        participate in mass
                                        executions.

Of course not. It's just . . .

                        I wasn't there.

They had nowhere to go.
It was frozen and hopeless.

                        They would never let him
                        leave.

He polished his gun over and over.

                        Oiled it, drilled, timed.

The dead gnawed on him.

                        He dragged himself through
                        battles, through villages
                        pockmarked by bombs.

They killed the survivors.

                        A single shot to the head.
                        He could taste their blood in
                        his mouth.

He could see their eyes, hear
their prayers.

                        He couldn't imagine the taste
                        of his mother's stew or her
                        bread, the boiled dandelions.

Couldn't remember the tree beside
his house that he used to climb.
Nothing.
It was snowing.

                                        They couldn't have fires.

He was trapped. The bombs
were getting closer.
The Americans approaching.

                                        He could be tried for murder
                                        by them or executed for
                                        desertion.

He didn't know what to do.

He stole a pistol, his image
reflected in it, distorted.

                                He cradled it in his mouth.

Powracać

Each soldier marched towards home,
carrying duty and ghosts like armor.
They buried the dead along the way,
throwing the bodies in trenches,
covering them with clay, trying to erase death.
The ones they did know were nameless, known
only by rank and race, vagabonds vanquished.
Gypsy curses hung before them like Hebrew prayer.

Matka Polka

to Czeslaw Milosz

I imagine you standing there
on a large wooden box
smiling.
The foreign crowds rush by you
speaking in French and German.
You begin to yell, daring them
to come closer. They watch you
carefully, as if you need pacifying, as if they can
ever still the anger. They nod occasionally,
pretending to understand.
This enrages you.
You taunt them,
mock them mocking you.
Who gave them the right to even
try understanding?
You scream out in Polish
into the throng of foreign tongues, hoping
that someone will call back. Your language is hiding—
like your people.

She was raped.
Her villages burned, her people
scattered. And for what?
Warsaw littered with the stench
of dead horses and ash,
the crying of old women heard
above the gunfire and rage.
You refused to defend her,
knowing it was too late, already
hearing Russians marching
and German guns.
You must have known

when you shook your head,
that the men who asked you
to join them, would all be dead.
Did you hear her screaming
in your poetry? Her terror?
Did you answer her cries,
silence them in your cadences?
Could you feel her trembling?
Were you like my great-grandfather?
Guilty?

Recording

Poland is about humanity losing itself.
Remnants of fabric, bone, loose coins,
a few beads. What remains of a life?
A ring, but it doesn't tell what the boy
whispered in her ear or how their hands touched.

Some Roman Catholic Poles did participate
both passively and actively. But not all of them.
Not all of them were in concentration camps either.

We all remember differently. The Germans didn't want
their history, neither did the Jews and Poles. And we're all left
with bitter ashes. Nothing is like it says in a textbook. Life
is muddled—filled with prejudices. When Pam, a Jewish woman,
speaks about seeing the Polish camps I am enraged. She touches
intimately what is mine. She, that also feels the anger, their pulses,
wears a cloak of faces and names. They whisper.

Years later, she and I are angry, a German woman lies awake
angry. We blame each other, roll our eyes, but we see
the faded pictures, the rain-rounded gravestones.
We call out the names.

To the Unknown Artist

It must have been 1940, a few days
before February 4th when they phoned you.
Nikolai Yezhov was not yet dead
but you knew he soon would be.
You got the call before Stalin,
an executioner yourself.
They gathered up pictures and photos,
handed you the box.
A gentle stroll with the Commissar turned
deadly on the banks of the Moscow-Volga Canal.
You with your tiny razor, pigment, paintbrush,
each stroke erasing his shadow, his hat, buttons,
you slowly smudged him into an inkblot,
dismantling flesh and bone, spirit.
A smile into waves, perfectly angled
reflections, a rebuilt wall.

Monologue of a Nazi/German Denier

So, I mean really. What were those Jews thinking? God—they never have been good at not getting their own way. Auschwitz didn't have gas chambers; there was no equipment to dispense gas. And if there was a gas mechanism, like the Jews said, it would have created a spark and ignited the Zyclon B. Obviously, the Jews were smart, but apparently not smart enough to know basic physics. That, or they underestimated our capacity for reason. There were no gas tight enclosures, and the piles of hair, obviously left behind for sanitary reasons; there were lice you know. And the shoes, please, those were obviously the Germans'. Why wouldn't they burn the shoes along with their supposed "victims"? And where the hell were the ashes put? Where are the 4,000,000 bodies or the 36,000,000 pounds of ashes? In the pond? Right . . . and the forensic data is where? Come on people, wake up, the Jews have obviously pulled a fast one on you. Of course, it's poor little ol' me, wah wah wah. Please, be serious. Gassings happened, sure, but not 6 million! And just because a few did occur, it doesn't mean that Nazi Germany was evil, or that Hitler wasn't God. The gas chambers were rebuilt by the Russians. Why don't you hear about the God damned Russians? It's them that killed us, and they killed more Jews than we ever did. Where are the autopsies? Prove that it was gas and the Germans! Prove it scientifically and analytically and maybe then I'll believe you, maybe. I used to believe the Holocaust stories, but now, look at the evidence, it's a hoax. The only gas chambers anywhere were delousing chambers used for clothing. And all of the survivors, please you know one person said one thing, and then they all decided to blame us. It was typhus not gas. What propaganda have you been fed? You're ignorant. The Americans and Jews wanted only to take away your will and give you shame.

Shoah

Pauline Aal 1872–1942
Rosa Aal 1888–1941
Siegfried Aal 1878–1941
Isidor Abraham 1871–1942
Julie Abraham 1878–1942
Werner Siegfried Abraham 1924–1941
Lucie Adelsberger 1895–1943
Elise Adler 1876–1941
Fanny Adler 1863–1942
Herman Adler 1882–?
Jakob Adler 1911–?
Josef Gabriel Adler 1924–?
Kurt Artur Adler 1915–?

Churban

A little boy stood there in the rain, the dirt beneath his bare feet turning to mud. He wore a tattered button-down coat, too small for even his small body and pants that were at his calves. He held his mother's hand, watching the line go forward slowly, inch-by-inch. It was rumored that liberation was just around the corner. His mother crossed herself as they took another step. There was a large bonfire a fair distance away and a closer table where a German soldier filled out forms. Each person was inspected and prodded towards the appropriate line. Those in the right-most line were being driven away in carts, their fate unknown, either shot away from the others, or going to labor camps, it was hard to tell. The middle line was being led towards a camp, forward to buildings and barbed wire. The third line, the longest, was heading towards the fire. The little boy wondered if it was warm by the orange glow. Dark smoke drifted upwards and he thought that it must be. They took another step, and another, until they were at the table. The little boy watched the man and he crossed himself like his mother did, quickly. The soldier scowled down at him, said something in a language that he couldn't understand and shoved them towards the line heading to the fire. The mother nodded at him, speaking quietly. They again waited for judgment. Eventually, they got to the fire. Watching carts of the dead being thrown into the blaze, watching the living jump in, those who had already seen their family killed footsteps in front of them. The woman took the boy's hand, watched the soldier, they could not jump, it would be a sin. The soldier yelled and the boy's mother shook her head trying to explain in Polish to the German what the problem was. In the end, he gave up frustrated, pushed them in, leaving only brass buttons.

Assemblage

"Whose book is this?" he asked, as he spied
World War II for Dummies. "This is just great!"
He picked it up, one hand caressing the cover
as the other opened it up excitedly fumbling.
And then he quickly looked up at me and blushed,
"Oh, yes, of course, it's yours."
And he was less enthusiastic, but only slightly,
I told him that he was right about the hedgerows.

Страстное желание

He had only wanted to see her again, just once
before winter. It was a fairly small wound,
nothing like shooting off a foot, just a bullet
to his right hand. He regretted it really,
but went to the medical tent anyway.
A doctor examined it closely,
when he called to another doctor,
he became nervous. The two doctors nodded,
declared it "self-inflicted" and called to a guard.
He was led outside, several members
of his battalion were called quickly together,
it was frigid, but very dry. He was told to strip,
called a coward. He stood at attention
facing the group. They watched him fall.

Чувство собственного достоинства

He'd been awarded the Red Star,
one of his comrades grabbed it from him,
showed it to the others that surrounded him,
then dropped it into a mug of Vodka with a plop.
He took the glass, toasted them, drained it quickly,
and smiled with it glittering between his teeth.

Routine

He sat in the dirt, leaning against his tank,
eyes sagging. He blinked at the mirror
attached to his machine gun.
He shaved, each stroke efficiently
scraping away the cream,
glanced blearily—the stubble was gone,
the exhaustion wasn't.

Russian Sniper

He watched from his hide
two Fritzs walking below.
They attempted to advance
unnoticed. They stared
at the body of his previous kill.
He smiled down at them,
hidden near a white wall,
the flash masked.
They crept along, almost crouching.
The Volga was freezing, the ice floes
colliding, grinding.
The soldiers glanced around nervously.
"Bam" one fell.
The other startled, hopped back slightly
then, he sank down, too.

In the Sunshine

They advanced through the prairie,
surrounded by soya beans and corn,
bodies strewn across the road,
a mixture of uniforms and blood
spattered rocks and leaves.
The wounded hid in the sunflowers.

Remembering

"You see, my letters were always kind of bland. My father was in World War I. I was going through his letters. I found out after that he was in the trenches. You know that it must have been hell—but he didn't write about any of that. Just the standard 'everything is fine here . . . hope all is well.' No one wants to worry the ones at home. They have enough to worry about. I always wrote about the scenery, the places I'd seen, the people I met. I didn't write about anything else. They didn't need to know about the time that I was put on duty because everyone was drunk, and I almost shot my own men. They didn't need to know about the terror I felt or the relief, when I heard them speaking English. They didn't need to know about bombs or the people in black and white stripes that kissed our feet. Those are things that you tell when you make it back safely, when years, and years have passed."

The Named

Hitler stared at the large map on the wall,
each advance outlined, flags progressing
deeper and deeper into Russia,
he was transfixed.

He folded his trembling hands, he nodded,
yes, I am a god.
This new beginning is my creation.

Stalin yelled for his staff—they stared at him,
wide eyed, as he yelled for "accurate" reports,
they nodded, lying, gritting their teeth.
They were not "panic mongers," just fathers.

Preparation

They dug, the dirt clinging to them,
caking onto them like a second skin,
the shovels were heavy.
It was October,
they could hear the enemy
approaching, a gentle snow began,
the women nodded to each other: winter.

Urban Archeology

I was in the library, cruising
through the used section,
looking for World War II books.
A man was perusing the same stack.
He glanced at me as I asked
if he'd seen a book that I wanted.
He shook his head no, glancing around.
He gave me a pointed look, asked
if the books were for me, or if there was a male
in the family that I was shopping for.
I shook my head, smiling, and said that they were for me.
He nodded and gave me the once over,
"You know," he said, "I've never met a woman
who was interested in war before."

Ambush

They waited, lying concealed
among heaps of straw,
a woman with red hair shouted orders,
grenades were thrown.
A Fritz would pass and fall quickly.
German soldiers paralyzed by women.

Rasputitsa Began

Rain made the land mud,
soldiers plodded along, legs
tired, heavy. A few jackboots
left behind, sucked in. It squished
and belched for miles. Dead Russians
were lined up in the mud,
used as planks, so that carts
could continue to roll.

Cierpienie

Near the forest of Katyn,
the Russians took their prisoners.
Officers, professors,
the unwanted and unneeded.
Hardened from war and beatings,
they were marched into ditches.
Thousands of rounds flew.
They fell like blowing leaves.
The dirt settled.

Sifting

A hand twists out through falling leaves,
a mound with fresh shovel prints,
the smell of rotting, blood
erupting from geysers in the summer heat.
The forest hides the bodies, each layer
of dirt holds more bone than rock.
How do you discover a mass grave?
Do you stumble over a loose shoe
or search for bones and bullets washed
upwards, shining eerily in the grass?

Разрушение

The German fighters began to carpet-bomb everything,
wooden houses went up in flame as incendiaries fell.
Everything was ash and smoke. The dead lay buried
beneath the rubble, the living scrambled to get into cellars
or ditches, the Volga's roar added to the sound of chaos.
Walls collapsed. The hospital crumbled. The dead mounted.

Miya-Jima

I stood on the island of Miya-Jima,
looking over the ocean from a look-out-point,
I thought Hiroshima would be a crater,
Instead, it looked alive, vibrant, with skyscrapers
and a skyline that rivaled New York's.
I was twelve and I didn't realize that I was crying until
tears splashed onto my travel brochure.
It was healing, like a forest taking back buildings,
moss and ivy slowly cracking stone,
rainwater and frost chipping away.
I ran up to the first Japanese girl I saw, Tatsumi.
I apologized for everything, the war, the bombs, death.
She nodded and smiled,
held out her index and middle finger in a V,
and said, "V for victory."

Mr. Yu

Age 85, winner of 8 Senior Olympic gold medals

He shook his head at me—"No, you don't understand,
war is terrible. I was in World War II. You know that, yes?
We had something to fight for—not like now.
The Japanese came over into China, they came over to kill us.
They were on our land—not like here.
Now, we kill without cause. War is terrible.
I was in China and there was this baby . . .
We had to take it from its mother. It was still sucking milk,
the baby was fine, but the mother was dead and the baby
was still sucking. And the worst thing I saw . . . the worst . . .
was when one of our planes crashed on the airfield.
They sent some workers, low ones, to pick up the body parts.
Each one was covered with white cloth and placed in the casket."

Reverberations

Write it down. Write it. With ordinary ink
—Wisława Szymborska, "Starvation Camp Near Jasło"

Read the names, read them one-by-one until
your breath gives way. Then sign them, K for Kim,
P for Pam . . . *What happens then? When you fall over
a root, but it's really a glove, when shattered glass
gives layers of meaning?* Lying on a floor of pine needles,
you can almost hear them. The rumbling tanks cracking
brush and branches. Men call out, the ground trembles.
I taste the mud that still clings to them. Say the names.
The ground is silent. The graves are only graves.
The water murmurs the song, ivy chokes the trees,
a bower for skeletons. Please. I cannot ask.
Let me taste it, feel it, breathe the bigness of it.
What do you become when you understand?

Author Notes

The word "Gypsy" is a slur word. In my work, I use the slur, and while it does address the Roma people, I hope that there is no disrespect taken. I attempt to use horrific words that were used during the time period to depict atrocities. Much of the language about homosexuality and ethnicity can be defined as slurs as well. My hope is to honor those individuals that lived the lives that I depict and who heard those words called to them. I ask forgiveness when they fall from my tongue at readings.

Title Translations

Najazd: Invasion (Polish)
Łamany: Broken (Polish)
Babushka: Grandmother (Polish)
Dziadek: Grandfather (Polish)
Rozgoryczenie: Bitterness/Resentment (Polish)
Trzy Tysiące Pięćset Sześćdziesiąt Trzy: Five hundred sixty-three thousand two hundred fifty-nine (Polish)
Obstrzał: Gunfire (Polish)
Nieznany: Unknown (Polish)
Kochanka: Mistress (Polish)
Żołnierze: Soldiers (Polish)
Soldaten: Soldiers (German)
Shwule: Gays (German)
Powracać: Return (Polish)
Matka Polka: Mother Poland (Polish)
Shoah: The Holocaust (Modern Hebrew)
Churban: The Destruction of First Temple and another word for Holocaust (Hebrew)
Страстное желание: Passionate Desire (Russian)
Чувство собственного достоинства: Self-Esteem, pride (Russian)
Rasputitsa Began: A mud storm, predictable (Russian)
Cierpienie: Suffering (Polish)
Разрушение: Destruction (Russian)

About the Author

Kim Malinowski is a lover of words. She earned her BA from West Virginia University and her MFA from American University. She is studying archeology and is the editor of the *ASM Ink,* the newsletter of the Archeological Society of Maryland.

She is the author of *Home* (Kelsay Books, 2021), *Phantom Reflection* (Silver Bow Publishing, 2022), *Buffy's House of Mirrors* (Q, an imprint of Querencia Press, 2023), *Clutching Narcissus* (Twelve House Books, 2024), and *Death: A Love Story* (Flutter Press, 2020).

Kim has been nominated for a Pushcart Prize, the Best of Net Award, and the Rhysling Award. She writes because the alternative is unthinkable.

www.ingramcontent.com/pod-product-compliance
Lightning Source LLC
Chambersburg PA
CBHW031204160426
43193CB00008B/496